baby animals

A PHOTOGRAPHIC CELEBRATION

2007 Metro Books

ISBN-13: 978-0-7607-9024-3
ISBN-10: 0-7607-9024-8

Printed and bound in Singapore

1   3   5   7   9   10   8   6   4   2

baby animals

A PHOTOGRAPHIC CELEBRATION

edited by marjorie galen

METRO BOOKS
NEW YORK

"There, in the center of the web,
neatly woven in block letters,
was a message. It said: SOME PIG!"
—E. B. WHITE

"Tyger! Tyger! burning bright,
In the forests of the night . . ."
—WILLIAM BLAKE

"Only YOU can prevent forest fires!"
—Smokey Bear, United States Forest Service mascot

Zebra stripes are like fingerprints; no two are alike.
Zoologists believe that this is how zebra mares and
their foals recognize each other in large herds.

For ages, man has asked the question: Which came first, the chicken or the egg? The earliest surviving mention of the problem came from first-century historian Plutarch.

"You look at any poetic creature: muslin, ether, demigoddess, millions of delights; then you look into the soul and find the most ordinary crocodile!"
—Anton Pavlovich Chekhov

"He was a good little monkey.
And always very curious."
—H. A. REY

"The early bird catcheth the worm."
—John Ray

"In the great forest a little elephant is born. His name is Babar."
—Jean de Brunhoff

"The trouble with a kitten is that
when it grows up, it's always a cat."
—Ogden Nash

"'I like this place,' said Mrs. Mallard
as they climbed out on the bank and waddled along."
—Robert McCloskey

"When you feel lousy, puppy therapy is indicated."
—Sara Paretsky

When a baby giraffe is born, its average height is six feet tall
and it weighs about 130 pounds.

"Yankee Doodle came to town
Riding on a pony;
Stuck a feather in his cap
And called it macaroni."
—Anonymous

"I never dreamed of so much happiness
when I was the Ugly Duckling!"
—HANS CHRISTIAN ANDERSEN

"An elephant's faithful, one hundred percent."
—Dr. Seuss

"It's better to be a lion for a day than a sheep all your life."
—Elizabeth Kenny

"We are just an advanced breed of monkeys
on a minor planet of a very average star. But we can understand the Universe.
That makes us something very special."
—Stephen Hawking

"No matter how much cats fight, there always seem to be plenty of kittens."
—Abraham Lincoln

"As for butter versus margarine, I trust cows more than chemists."
—Joan Gussow

Frogs don't drink. They absorb the water they need through their skin.

"Don't count your chickens before they are hatched."
—Aesop

Psychologists at the University of Leicester in the United Kingdom found that dairy cows produce more milk—3 percent more per cow—when listening to calming music. The cows were big fans of the mellow sounds of Beethoven and Simon and Garfunkel, but refused to pump out the excess volume for more raucous music.

Even though most birds spend much of their time crisscrossing the blue skies, owls are the only birds that can see the color blue.

"If a picture wasn't going very well I'd put a puppy dog in it, always a mongrel, you know, never one of the full-bred puppies. And then I'd put a bandage on its foot . . . I liked it when I did it, but now I'm sick of it."
—Norman Rockwell

Black and white doesn't look like camouflage to our eyes because we see in color. But for zebras, their stripes help them blend in, and stay safe from predators, because their enemies see only in black and white.

"Alice came to a fork in the road. 'Which road do I take?' she asked. 'Where do you want to go?' responded the Cheshire cat. 'I don't know,' Alice answered. 'Then,' said the cat, 'it doesn't matter.'"

—LEWIS CARROLL

Baby elephants weigh as much as 500 pounds.

The ancient Egyptians, who worshipped felines thousands of years ago, were the first to domesticate the cat. Paintings in pharaohs' tombs show pictures of cats as royal pets.

"Always behave like a duck—
keep calm and unruffled on the surface
but paddle like the devil underneath."
—JACOB BRAUDE

A lion's roar is very loud, and can be heard from as far as five miles away.

Polar bears have fur on the bottom of their paws to provide traction on the ice.

Elephants bear their young 22 months after conception, making their gestation period the longest of any land animal.

"The key to everything is patience. You get the chicken by hatching the egg—not by smashing it."
—ARNOLD GLASOW

The fastest animal in the world is a bird.
The peregrine falcon can fly at speeds
of up to 200 miles per hour.

A grizzly bear standing on its hind legs is an impressive
and frightening sight, but the bear might just be curious
and trying to get a better view of the action.

Giraffes are silent because they have no vocal chords.

"It is impossible to keep a straight face in the presence of one or more kittens."
—CYNTHIA E. VARNADO

Koala fingerprints appear to be human. A koala's prints at a crime scene might even confuse the police.

"A camel makes an elephant feel like a jet plane."
—JACQUELINE KENNEDY

Penguins live only in the southern hemisphere.

"Everyone wants to understand painting. Why is there no attempt
to understand the song of the birds?"
—PABLO PICASSO

"Dogs look up to us. Cats look down at us. Pigs treat us as equals."
—Winston Churchill

On a 1902 hunting trip, President Theodore "Teddy" Roosevelt refused to shoot a defenseless bear. Political cartoonist Clifford Berryman immortalized the event with a cartoon of the president sparing the life of a frightened cub.
Teddy's Bear, as the president's political mascot was known,
boosted Roosevelt's popularity and inspired the first stuffed teddy bear.

Some penguins build stone nests
and the male and female take turns keeping their chicks
warm and safe while the other searches for food.

"My Christmas will be a whole lot wetter and merrier
if somebody sends me a six-week-old Boston terrier."
—E. B. White

Giant pandas weigh well more than 200 pounds when fully grown,
but a newborn is only the size of a stick of butter.

Early explorers in the Antarctic thought that penguins were fish, not birds. Penguins don't fly through the air, but they do "fly" through the water at speeds of up to 25 miles per hour.

"Behold the turtle.
He makes progress only when he sticks his neck out."
—James Bryant Conant

The American Society for the Prevention of Cruelty to Animals (ASPCA) surveyed veterinarians to find out what the most popular pet names in the United States are today. Max, Sam, and Lady were the top three.

You're not alone if you live with a cat.
Cats are the most popular pets in the United States today.
Dogs follow in second place.

"A new-born calf fears not the tiger"
—CHINESE PROVERB

The word *raccoon* comes from an Algonquin Indian word that means "he scratches with his hands." In fact, this is a very appropriate name since a raccoon's paws are extremely good at opening things, especially garbage-can lids.

A chimpanzee's genetic material differs by only 1.6 percent from that of humans, making chimps our closest relatives.

"You enter into a certain amount of madness
when you marry a person with pets."
—NORA EPHRON

Although black cats are regarded with superstition in America, in other parts of the world, such as Asia and England, a black cat is considered lucky.

Considering that a full-grown hippopotamus weighs up to three-and-a-half tons, it shouldn't be a surprise that a newborn hippo can weigh as much as 120 pounds.

An elephant calf sucks its trunk for comfort,
just as a human baby sucks its thumb.

"Happiness is a warm puppy."
—Charles M. Schulz

A zebra is a light-colored animal with dark stripes,
not a dark one with light stripes.

"It is a very inconvenient habit of kittens (Alice had once made the remark) that, whatever you say to them, they always purr."
—LEWIS CARROLL

A baby chimpanzee spends the first few months of life clinging
to its mother's belly. Even when it can travel on its own,
the young chimpanzee will spend as many as 10 years with its mother
learning how to be a chimp—grooming, nesting, finding food, and using tools.

"There is something about the outside of a horse
that is good for the inside of a man."
—WINSTON CHURCHILL

"A wise old owl lived in an oak;
The more he heard, the less he spoke;
The less he spoke, the more he heard.
Oh, if men were all like that wise old bird!"
—*Punch*

Often called the king of the jungle, the lion actually lives on plains and in woodlands, not in the forest.

"Some of my best leading men have been dogs and horses."
—ELIZABETH TAYLOR

Humans first domesticated sheep about 10,000 years ago, and today there are more than 200 different varieties.

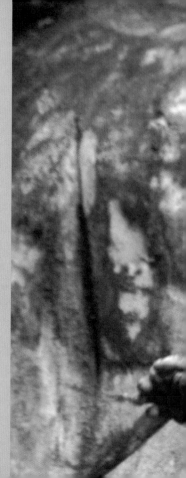

The chimpanzee's arms are so long that they reach below its knees.

"The Owl and the Pussy-Cat went to sea
In a beautiful pea-green boat.
They took some honey and plenty of money,
Wrapped up in a five-pound note."
—EDWARD LEAR

"Tigers do not sire puppy-dogs."
—CHINESE PROVERB

New Zealand is home to more than 40 million sheep and only about 4 million people. That's 10 sheep per person.

Owls swallow their prey whole and later throw up whatever they can't digest in the form of pellets.

"Whoever said you can't buy happiness forgot little puppies."
—GENE HILL

Elephants keep up their weight by eating
as much as 300 pounds of food per day.

"Cats are the ultimate narcissists. You can tell this because of all the time they spend on personal grooming. Dogs aren't like this. A dog's idea of personal grooming is to roll on a dead fish."
—James Gorman

"If I had to choose, I would rather have birds than airplanes."
—CHARLES A. LINDBERGH

The tiger is the largest and most powerful member of the cat family.
Despite the fact that an adult male can weigh more than one third of a ton,
the tiger stalks its prey almost silently, getting close enough to pounce.

"An appeaser is one who feeds a crocodile—hoping it will eat him last."
—Winston Churchill

About 200 million scent receptors fill a fox's nose—
that's 40 times the measly 5 million in the human nose.
Something to think about when walking past a pile of garbage.

"If I didn't start painting, I would have raised chickens."
—GRANDMA MOSES

"If you are a dog and your owner suggests that you wear a sweater . . . suggest that he wear a tail."
—FRAN LEBOWITZ

An owl has very large eyes that fill more than half its skull—
the better to see at night. Its eyes don't move in their sockets;
instead, the owl is able to turn its head three-quarters of the way
around, look over either shoulder, and see behind as well as in front.

"I am impelled, not to squeak like a grateful and
apologetic mouse, but to roar like a lion
out of pride in my profession."
—JOHN STEINBECK

People often make the mistake of thinking that a koala is a kind of bear.
Actually, the koala is a marsupial—like the kangaroo—and has a pouch to carry its young.
The koala's pouch opens to the rear of the body, so that the opening faces the ground
when the koala is upright. This sounds like it could be a problem,
but luckily the young koalas don't fall out.

"God has created the cat
to give man the pleasure of caressing the tiger."
—Theophile Gautier

Tigers don't have just striped fur;
the stripes are on their skin as well.

Kangaroos are extremely powerful and fast,
running up to 35 miles per hour and
taking leaps the length of two cars.

"The creatures outside looked from pig to man,
and from man to pig, and from pig to man again;
but already it was impossible to say which was which."
—George Orwell

Every night, the chimpanzee builds a new sleeping nest in the trees.
The nest, built from twigs and leaves, takes the chimpanzee only five minutes to construct and helps to keep it safe from enemies. Young chimpanzees learn nest-making from their mothers.

"If you can dream it, you can do it. Always remember this whole thing was started by a mouse."
—WALT DISNEY

Emperor penguins hang out in large groups,
using their body heat to keep warm. The penguins take turns being on the outside,
where it's cold, and getting a chance to warm up in the center,
where they're protected from the frigid Antarctic wind.

Golden retriever puppies have lighter coats than adults.

People are sometimes said to "breed like rabbits"
if they have a lot of children, but it would be impossible to truly keep up.
Female rabbits have up to 9 kittens in each litter,
and up to 30 young in a single year.

"No bird soars too high if he soars with his own wings."
—WILLIAM BLAKE

"The one-*l* lama,
He's a priest.
The two-*l* llama,
He's a beast."
—Ogden Nash

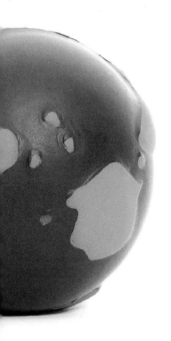

"As they were poor, owing to the amount of milk the children drank, this nurse was a prim Newfoundland dog, called Nana, who belonged to no one in particular until the Darlings engaged her."
—J. M. Barrie

Contrary to myth,
a goat is particular about what it consumes
and won't ingest a tin can.

"But the wildest of all wild animals was the cat. He walked by himself, and all places were alike to him."
—Rudyard Kipling

"It is not only fine feathers that make fine birds."
—Aesop

"It is a blind goose that cometh to the fox's sermon."
—JOHN LYLY

"After *Wizard of Oz*, I was typecast as a lion,
and there just aren't that many roles for lions in Hollywood."
—BERT LAHR

"He respects Owl, because you can't help respecting anybody who can spell TUESDAY, even if he doesn't spell it right; but spelling isn't everything. "
—A. A. MILNE

No one knows why, but the raccoon has the rare habit
of washing its food before eating.

"In order to see birds, it is necessary to become part of the silence."
—ROBERT LYND

"And the only reason for being a bee that I know of
is making honey. And the only reason I know
for making honey is so as I can eat it."
—Winnie-the-Pooh

Some experts think that pigs are more trainable than dogs and cats.

"If you are losing a tug of war with a tiger,
give him the rope before he gets to your arm.
You can always buy a new rope."
—Max Gunther

A horse's height is not measured in inches, but in hands.
One hand equals about four inches, and the horse is measured from the ground
to the ridge between the shoulders, known as the withers.

"I am a Bear of Very Little Brain and long words Bother me."
—Winnie-the-Pooh

At birth, a baby koala is very small—about the size of a jelly bean. The joey then spends the first six months of its life in its mother's pouch.

"The bluebird carries the sky on his back."
—Henry David Thoreau

"Did you think the lion was sleeping because he didn't roar?"
—Johann Friedrich von Schiller

"Some cats chase mice. I prefer to take legal action."
—GARFIELD THE CAT

Grizzly bear mothers need enough stored fat to sustain themselves
and their embryos through the long winter,
or else the embryos won't develop.

"Monkeys very sensibly refrain from speech
lest they should be set to earn their livings."
—KENNETH GRAHAME

Man is the rhinoceros's only predator.
Because of human hunting practices, the rhino is endangered.

"Ever consider what they must think of us? I mean, here we come back from a grocery store with the most amazing haul—chicken, pork, half a cow . . . they must think we're the greatest hunters on Earth!"
—ANNE TYLER

"So long, and thanks for all the fish."
—Douglas Adams

It's easy to find the Ursa Major, or Great Bear, constellation because its seven brightest stars make up the Big Dipper.

Meerkats, like all members of the mongoose family, are immune to many venoms. They can eat many snakes and scorpions without fear of sickness or death.

"For every Bear that ever there was
Will gather there for certain because
Today's the day the Teddy Bears have their Picnic."
—JOHN W. BRATTON AND JAMES B. KENNEDY

Earless seals are much more comfortable in the water. On land, because their hind flippers don't turn downward, they have to move around by wriggling with their front flippers and abdominal muscles.

"God loved the birds and invented trees.
Man loved the birds and invented cages."
—JACQUES DEVAL

Chimpanzees use more tools than any other animal besides humans. They use long grass to "fish" in termite nests, sticks and stones as weapons to throw or wield, and stones as hammers to crack open nuts.

"Spirituality is like a bird:
If you hold it too closely, it chokes,
And if you hold it too loosely, it escapes."
—Israel Salanter Lipkin

Moose eat saplings and shrubs and are named for the Algonquian word *mus* or *mooz,* meaning "twig eater."

"Being a president is like riding a tiger . . . keep on riding or be swallowed."
—HARRY S TRUMAN

"The majority of husbands remind me of an orangutan trying to play the violin."
—Honoré de Balzac

During the nineteenth century in the United States, train conductors had to keep an eye out for bison herds, which caused damage to the locomotives (and the bison) if the trains were unable to stop in time.

"The quizzical expression of the monkey at the zoo comes from his wondering whether he is his brother's keeper or his keeper's brother."
—Evan Esar

"There are two lasting bequests we can give our children:
one is roots. The other is wings."
—HODDING CARTER JR.

Kangaroo babies, called joeys, are born at a very early state of development— after just over 30 days of gestation. After birth, they use their partly developed forelimbs to climb into the mother's pouch and attach to a teat. A joey stays in the pouch for about nine months before beginning to venture out.

"Depend on the rabbit's foot if you will,
but remember it didn't work for the rabbit."
—R. E. Shay

"It matters nothing if one is born in a duck-yard, if one has only lain in a swan's egg."
—HANS CHRISTIAN ANDERSEN

"Crazy like a fox."
—S. J. PERELMAN

Barn owls can be found in the wild on every continent except Antarctica.

"You may as well say, that's a valiant flea
that dare eat his breakfast on the lip of a lion."
—WILLIAM SHAKESPEARE

The Beach Boys' 1967 *Smiley Smile* album featured a song named for everyone's favorite cartoon woodpecker and entitled "Fall Breaks and Back to Winter (Woody Woodpecker Symphony)."

"The song of canaries
Never varies,
And when they're moulting
They're pretty revolting."
—Ogden Nash

Elephants use their trunks to keep cool and hydrated in the hot sun. The elephant can suck as much as two gallons of water into its trunk at a time, and can then either blow the water into its own mouth or squirt it over its body to keep cool.

"If animals could speak, the dog would be a blundering outspoken fellow; but the cat would have the rare grace of never saying a word too much."
—MARK TWAIN

A famous African gray parrot named N'Kisi is said to have a vocabulary of 950 words and to understand how to make a joke. Alex Kirby, of the BBC News online, reported: "When he first met Dr Jane Goodall, the renowned chimpanzee expert, after seeing her in a picture with apes, N'kisi said: 'Got a chimp?'"

White lions are rare because their coloring
is the result of a recessive gene. Unlike regular lions,
a white lion doesn't blend into its surroundings
and is more easily spotted by hunters as well as its own prey.

Although the hunter never appeared on the screen
in Walt Disney's *Bambi,* Man was named number 20 in the
American Film Institute's top-50 greatest movie villains for his role in the film.

" It does not matter a hoot what the mockingbird
is singing. . . . The real and proper question is: Why is it beautiful?"
—ANNIE DILLARD

All cats directly register; that is, when they walk they place their hind paws almost directly in the prints of their forepaws. Walking this way helps cats to navigate difficult terrain, to sneak up quietly on their prey, and to leave fewer visible tracks.

"... And on his farm, he had some chicks. E-I-E-I-O.
With a *chick, chick* here and a *chick, chick* there;
here a *chick,* there a *chick,* everywhere a *chick-chick.*"
—"OLD MCDONALD HAD A FARM"

In 1877, Thomas Edison recited the first stanza of "Mary Had a Little Lamb," by Sarah Hale in order to test his invention of the phonograph. Hence, the story of little Mary and her ever-present lamb was the subject of the first successful audio recording in history.

"My purpose is, indeed, a horse of that colour."
—WILLIAM SHAKESPEARE

"Keep your sense of humor. As General Joe Stillwell said,
'The higher a monkey climbs, the more you see of his behind.'"
—DONALD RUMSFELD

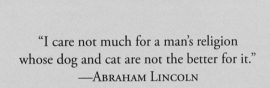

"I care not much for a man's religion
whose dog and cat are not the better for it."
—Abraham Lincoln

"The coachman was instructed to purchase for him
the handsomest pony which could be bought for money."
—*Vanity Fair*

"Cats are intended to teach us that not everything in nature has a purpose."
—GARRISON KEILLOR

"Bring me a bowl of coffee before I turn into a goat."
—Johann Sebastian Bach

Mother cheetahs will leave their cubs when the young ones are 18 months old, but the siblings will stick together, sometimes for life.

"I learned the way a monkey learns—by watching its parents."
—CHARLES, PRINCE OF WALES

Capricorns, born from December 22 through January 19, are represented astrologically by the goat. For those who believe in astrology, the goat, who loves to get to the top of the mountain, is an apt mascot for the determined and ambitious Capricorn.

Baseball Hall of Famer Orlando Cepeda is nicknamed "The Baby Bull," after his father, Puerto Rican baseball legend Pedro Cepeda, whose nickname is "The Bull."

"I know why the caged bird sings."
—MAYA ANGELOU

"At the turn of the century, at least one, possibly two million, chimpanzees were present in 25 countries across West and Central Africa. Now, only four countries have significant populations of chimpanzees, and probably no more than 150,000 chimpanzees are left across all of Africa."
—THE JANE GOODALL INSTITUTE

In 1974, British progressive rock band Genesis released their sixth studio album, *The Lamb Lies Down on Broadway.*

"We should be careful to get out of an experience only the wisdom that is in it—
and stop there; lest we be like the cat that sits down on a hot stove-lid.
She will never sit down on a hot stove-lid again, and that is well;
but also she will never sit down on a cold one anymore."
—MARK TWAIN

"Wooing the press is an exercise roughly akin to picnicking with a tiger. You might enjoy the meal, but the tiger always eats last."
—MAUREEN DOWD

"If you want a kitten, start out asking for a horse."
—ANONYMOUS

"A bird in the hand is a certainty, but a bird in the bush may sing."
—BRET HARTE

"Wild horses couldn't drag me away."
—TRADITIONAL SAYING

The nickname "Cubs" was first given to the Chicago baseball team by a *Chicago Daily News* reporter in 1902. The manager at the time, Frank Selee, inspired the name by his choice of young, inexperienced players to rebuild the team. The name stuck and was officially adopted by the team in 1907.

"The most appealing and intriguing thing about [Donald Duck] was his voice, supplied by Clarence Nash. It was said that Walt Disney himself had heard Nash on a local radio station reciting 'Mary Had a Little Lamb' and, fascinated by the voice, ordered him to be hired."
—RON GOULART

Young deer can be called "fawns" or "calves."

"Winston Churchill is always expecting rabbits to come out of an empty hat."
—Evelyn Waugh

A lamb drinks its mother's milk for about four months,
and then it moves on to solids, eating grass,
hay, and grain, and drinking water.

Fox babies are called "kits."

"Stealing a rhinoceros should not be attempted lightly."
—KEHLOG ALBRAN

"I do not know which to prefer,
The beauty of inflections
Or the beauty of innuendos,
The blackbird whistling
Or just after."
—WALLACE STEVENS

"Don't approach a goat from the front,
a horse from the back, or a fool from any side."
—YIDDISH PROVERB

For thousands of years, cheetahs have been tamed by man to be kept as pets or trained to help with hunting.

"A really companionable and indispensable dog is an accident of nature.
You can't get it by breeding for it, and you can't buy it with money. It just happens along."
—E. B. WHITE

Lynx are relatively small, but have very large feet.
A 30-pound lynx has larger feet than a 20-pound mountain lion.
Their big feet act like snowshoes, helping the animal to hunt in deep snow.

"The biggest dog has been a pup."
—Joaquin Miller

"For want of a nail, the shoe was lost;
for want of a shoe, the horse was lost;
for want of a horse, the rider was lost;
for want of a rider, the battle was lost;
for want of a battle, the kingdom was lost,
and all for the want of a horse-shoe nail."
—Anonymous

"Use what talents you possess;
the woods would be very silent if no birds sang
except those that sang best."
—HENRY VAN DYKE

Lemurs are native only to Madagascar (an island off the coast of Africa) and the Comoro Islands.

"Operationally, God is beginning to resemble not a ruler
but the last fading smile of a cosmic Cheshire cat."
—Sir Julian Huxley

"God is really only another artist.
He invented the giraffe, the elephant, and the cat.
He has no real style. He just keeps on trying other things."
—PABLO PICASSO

"When there is no tiger on the mountain, the monkey becomes king."
—CHINESE PROVERB

The word *jaguar* comes from the South American word *yagura,* meaning "wild beast that overcomes its prey with a single bound."

Hedgehogs are covered with quills—5,000 to 7,000 of them—
that are hard on the outside, but not very sharp. To protect itself
from predators, the hedgehog uses two large muscles on its
back to raise and lower its quills, and to curl into a ball.

"Distance tests a horse's strength. Time reveals a person's character."
—CHINESE PROVERB

Hares can run as fast as 50 miles per hour—
especially when being chased! The hare will zig, zag, and jump
in the air in order to throw its predators off the trail.

American president Thomas Jefferson had a great appreciation for mockingbirds. His pet mockingbird, Dick, flew freely around his study at the White House.

"Bah, bah, black sheep,
have you any wool?
Yes sir, yes sir,
three bags full."
—Traditional nursery rhyme

"A great many people now reading and writing
would be better employed in keeping rabbits."
—DAME EDITH SITWELL

Pumas, or cougars as they are also known, are strong cats—
they can kill and drag prey up to seven times their own weight.

"That which is called firmness in a king
is called obstinacy in a donkey."
—John Erskine

"I do not believe that any peacock envies another peacock his tail, because every peacock is persuaded that his own tail is the finest in the world. The consequence of this is that peacocks are peaceable birds."
—John Ruskin

"Hark to the whimper of the seagull.
He weeps because he's not an ea-gull.
Suppose you were, you silly seagull.
Could you explain it to your she-gull?"
—Ogden Nash

"If man could be crossed with the cat, it would improve man but deteriorate the cat."
—MARK TWAIN

A cow doesn't produce milk until after giving birth.
In fact, a cow is not even called a cow until it becomes a mother.
Before that, the female calf is known as a heifer.
Farmers breed their heifers at about 15 months of age,
and they give birth approximately 9 months later.

"A strange white heron rising with silver on its wings,
Rising and crying
Wordless, wondrous things."
—William Rose Benét

Adult male swans are called "cobs" and adult females are called "pens."

"The crow wished everything was black, the owl, that every thing was white."
—William Blake

"It will be a lovely knee-high black-and-white penguin waddling up the snow-covered beach that will steal your heart."
—Lloyd Spencer Davis

"When it comes to having a central nervous system, and the ability to feel pain, hunger, and thirst, a rat is a pig is a dog is a boy."
—INGRID NEWKIRK

"I hope you love birds too. It is economical. It saves going to heaven."
—EMILY DICKINSON

The word *koala* is thought to mean "no drink" in the Aboriginal language. It's true—koalas get most of the water they need from eating leaves, and only rarely drink water.

"Weaseling out of things is important to learn.
It's what separates us from the animals . . . except the weasel."
—MATT GROENING

"Pussycat, pussycat, where have you been?
I've been to London to visit the Queen. "
—Traditional nursery rhyme

Unlike pythons, baby boas hatch inside their moms.
The boa is ovoviviparous, meaning it carries its fertilized eggs
within its body, eventually giving birth to live young.

"You cannot fly like an eagle with the wings of a wren."
—WILLIAM HENRY HUDSON

Alpacas have been valued for their soft and lustrous wool for thousands of years; wool spun from the alpaca is stronger than sheep's wool.

Donkeys mature slowly, sometimes not reaching full physical maturity until six years of age.

"When you have got an elephant by the hind legs and he is trying to run away, it's best to let him run."
—ABRAHAM LINCOLN

"All of us are guinea pigs in the laboratory of God.
Humanity is just a work in progress."
—Tennessee Williams

Baby skunks, which are usually born in May, leave their mothers in July or August.

"I value my garden more for being full of blackbirds
than of cherries, and very frankly give them fruit for their songs."
—JOSEPH ADDISON

"Doggy, doggy, where's your bone?
Somebody stole it from your home!"
—ENGLISH NURSERY RHYME

"How doth the little crocodile
Improve his shining tail,
And pour the waters of the Nile
On every golden scale!"
—LEWIS CARROLL

A three-month-old tern was observed flying almost 14,000 miles in one journey—one of the longest bird flights ever recorded.

"A horse is dangerous at both ends and uncomfortable in the middle."
—Ian Fleming

"You can't catch a cub without going into the tiger's den."
—CHINESE PROVERB

"Until one has loved an animal,
a part of one's soul remains unawakened."
—ANATOLE FRANCE

"It's not easy being green."
—KERMIT THE FROG

Cheetahs can run up to 70 miles per hour,
making them the fastest mammal in the world.
Found in Africa and Asia, these beautiful cats are
increasingly rare and in danger of extinction.

Two fingerlike muscles on the tip allow the elephant
to use its trunk to pluck a single leaf from a tree,
or even pick a pin up off the ground.

"A barking dog is often more useful than a sleeping lion."
—Washington Irving

"When Mrs. Frederick C. Little's second son arrived,
everybody noticed that he was not much bigger
than a mouse. The truth of the matter was, the baby looked
very much like a mouse in every way."
—E. B. WHITE

Turtles are known for their longevity. The smaller species can live more than 30 years, and some of the giant tortoises in captivity are thought to be over 200 years old.

"Every animal knows more than you do."
—Native American proverb

"Never hold discussions with the monkey
when the organ grinder is in the room."
—WINSTON CHURCHILL

Lions can run fast—up to 50 miles per hour.
But like any self-respecting house cat, they also like to relax,
and spend as much as 20 hours per day resting.

"Oh my fur and whiskers!"
—Lewis Carroll

"Know yourself. Don't accept your dog's admiration as conclusive evidence that you are wonderful."
—ANN LANDERS

"Who was the first guy that looked at a cow
and said, 'I think that I'll drink whatever comes out
of those things when I squeeze them'?"
—BILL WATTERSON

"The groundhog is like most other prophets;
it delivers its prediction and then disappears."
—BILL VAUGHN

"Meerkats stand tall; as adults they're barely a foot tall, even on tiptoe. But if helpfulness equaled height, meerkats would be giants. Nearly a decade of fieldwork in South Africa by my international team shows meerkats to be among the most cooperative mammals on Earth. *Homo sapiens* come close, but only on our best days."

—TIM CLUTTON-BROCK

Turtles have been around since the time of the dinosaurs, and currently live on every continent except Antarctica. The different species—270 in total—vary in size from the 4-inch speckled cape tortoise to the 96-inch leatherback sea turtle.

"If happiness truly consisted in physical ease and freedom from care,
the happiest individual would not be either a man or a woman, but an American cow."
—WILLIAM LYON PHELPS

"A gray baboon sits statue-like alone
Watching the sunrise; while on lower boughs
His puny offspring leap about and play."
—Toru Dutt

"If March comes in like a lion, it'll go out like a lamb.
If it comes in like a lamb, it'll go out like a lion."
—ENGLISH PROVERB

"I believe that these sea lions that are washing up along the coast are actually acting as important canaries in the coal mine, warning us of some ocean changes that contribute in fact to human health."
—FRANCES GULLAND

"Of all the things I miss from veterinary practice, puppy breath is one of the most fond memories!"
—Dr. Tom Cat

"The reason birds can fly and we can't is simply that
they have perfect faith,
for faith is necessary to have wings."
—James M. Barrie

In 1783, a sheep, a duck, and a rooster
were given the first ride ever in a hot air balloon.
It was a short ride—the balloon only stayed aloft
for 15 minutes—before plummeting down to the ground.

"A dog too, had he; not for need,
But one to play with and to feed;"
—WILLIAM WORDSWORTH

"You can put wings on a pig,
but you don't make it an eagle."
—BILL CLINTON

Black bear cubs cry when they're hungry or cold and purr when they've been fed.

"She shall be sportive as the fawn
That wild with glee across the lawn."
—WILLIAM WORDSWORTH

"Blackbird has spoken
Like the first bird."
—Eleanor Farjeon

"There once was a brainy baboon
Who always breathed down a bassoon.
For he said, 'It appears
That in billions of years
I shall certainly hit on a tune.'"
—Ezra Pound

Until the nineteenth century, as many as 60 million bison lived on the Great Plains from Mexico into Canada, and some were found east of the Mississippi River. They were central to the existence of the Plains peoples, who used them for food, hides, and bone implements; even the dried dung, called buffalo chips, was used as fuel.

"He was so learned that he could name a horse in nine languages;
so ignorant that he bought a cow to ride on."
—BENJAMIN FRANKLIN

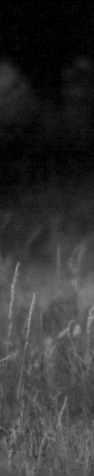

"A hen is only an egg's way of making another egg."
—Samuel Butler

The American opossum has the shortest gestation period in the animal kingdom, giving birth to its young just 12 to 13 days after conception.

Raccoons can lose as much as 50 percent of their body weight over the course of the winter.

"I think mice
Are rather nice."
—ROSE FYLEMAN

"In order to really enjoy a dog, one doesn't merely try to train him to be semihuman. The point of it is to open oneself to the possibility of becoming partly a dog."
—EDWARD HOAGLAND

Baby swans are called "cygnets."

Two-hump camels, known as Bactrian camels, have an inner coat of down that can be spun into yarn for knitting.

"Now I know that much of parenthood is watching and waiting
for the chick to fall into harm's way, watching and waiting for the cats and the cold nights.
The joyous enterprise has an undercurrent of terror."
—ANNA QUINDLEN

Sheep and goats have horizontal slit-shaped pupils. This shape improves their depth perception on the vertical plane, and helps them to navigate in mountainous environments.

"One day I was walking through the jungle and I shot an elephant in my pajamas. How he got in my pajamas, I'll never know."
—GROUCHO MARX

Sometimes even a giraffe's long neck isn't long enough to reach
the good parts of the tree. The giraffe extends its reach with its long, prehensile tongue,
which is blue-black in color to protect it from sunburn.

"Yesterday I was a dog. Today I'm a dog. Tomorrow I'll probably still be a dog. Sigh! There's so little hope for advancement."
—Snoopy

The Beluga whale, or white whale as it is sometimes known,
may have gotten its name from the Russian words *beloye* or *belukha,*
meaning "white" or "white one."

"Buy a pup and your money will buy love unflinching."
—RUDYARD KIPLING

"All animals are equal
but some animals are more equal than others."
—GEORGE ORWELL

PHOTOGRAPHY CREDITS

The following abbreviations are used: JI—© 2007 Jupiter Images Corporation; BS—Big Stock Photo; iSP—iStockphoto.com; IO—www.indexopen.com; SS—ShutterStock

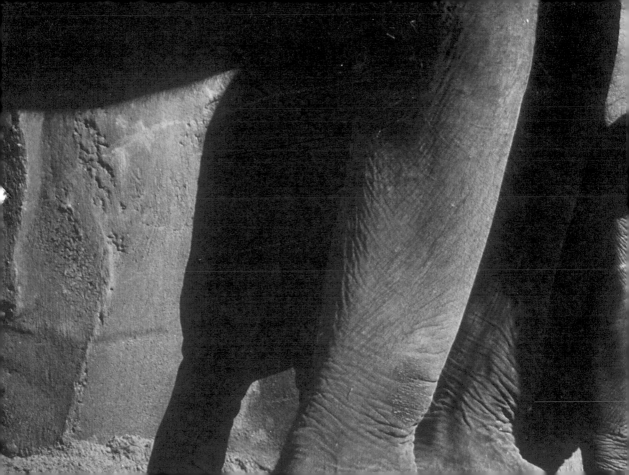